50 Sweet Potato Meal Recipes

By: Kelly Johnson

Table of Contents

- Baked Sweet Potatoes with Cinnamon and Brown Sugar
- Sweet Potato Casserole with Marshmallows
- Sweet Potato and Black Bean Tacos
- Mashed Sweet Potatoes with Garlic
- Sweet Potato and Kale Frittata
- Sweet Potato Quinoa Bowl
- Roasted Sweet Potato Salad with Feta
- Sweet Potato and Chickpea Curry
- Sweet Potato Gnocchi with Sage Butter
- Sweet Potato and Bacon Hash
- Sweet Potato Fries with Chipotle Mayo
- Stuffed Sweet Potatoes with Spinach and Feta
- Sweet Potato Soup with Coconut Milk
- Sweet Potato Pancakes
- Sweet Potato and Lentil Stew
- Sweet Potato Gratin with Gruyère
- Sweet Potato Waffles with Maple Syrup
- Sweet Potato and Apple Bake
- Sweet Potato and Sausage Skillet
- Sweet Potato Risotto with Parmesan
- Sweet Potato Pizza with Goat Cheese
- Sweet Potato and Corn Chowder
- Sweet Potato Hash Brown Casserole
- Sweet Potato and Chicken Enchiladas
- Sweet Potato Burgers with Avocado
- Sweet Potato Salad with Apples and Pecans
- Spicy Sweet Potato Hummus
- Sweet Potato Tater Tot Casserole
- Sweet Potato and Broccoli Stir-Fry
- Sweet Potato and Shrimp Stir-Fry
- Sweet Potato Chilaquiles
- Sweet Potato and Spinach Stuffed Shells
- Sweet Potato and Turkey Meatballs
- Grilled Sweet Potato Skewers
- Sweet Potato Sushi Rolls
- Sweet Potato Chocolate Chip Cookies

- Sweet Potato Pudding
- Sweet Potato and Mushroom Risotto
- Sweet Potato and Green Bean Salad
- Sweet Potato Muffins
- Baked Sweet Potato and Egg Breakfast Bowls
- Sweet Potato Chocolate Brownies
- Sweet Potato and Coconut Curry
- Sweet Potato and White Bean Chili
- Sweet Potato and Cauliflower Tacos
- Sweet Potato and Zucchini Fritters
- Sweet Potato and Brussels Sprouts Salad
- Sweet Potato Mac and Cheese
- Sweet Potato and Roasted Beet Salad
- Sweet Potato Chocolate Mousse

Baked Sweet Potatoes with Cinnamon and Brown Sugar

Ingredients:

- 4 medium sweet potatoes
- 2 tablespoons unsalted butter
- 2 tablespoons brown sugar
- 1 teaspoon cinnamon
- Salt to taste

Instructions:

1. Preheat your oven to 400°F (200°C).
2. Wash and pierce sweet potatoes with a fork. Place them on a baking sheet.
3. Bake for 45-60 minutes or until tender.
4. Let them cool slightly, then slice open and fluff the insides with a fork.
5. Add butter, brown sugar, cinnamon, and salt. Mix well and serve warm.

Sweet Potato Casserole with Marshmallows

Ingredients:

- 4 cups mashed sweet potatoes
- 1/2 cup brown sugar
- 1/4 cup milk
- 1/4 cup unsalted butter, melted
- 1 teaspoon vanilla extract
- 2 cups mini marshmallows

Instructions:

1. Preheat oven to 350°F (175°C).
2. In a large bowl, combine mashed sweet potatoes, brown sugar, milk, melted butter, and vanilla.
3. Transfer to a greased baking dish and smooth the top.
4. Bake for 25 minutes. Remove from oven and top with mini marshmallows.
5. Return to the oven for an additional 10-15 minutes, until marshmallows are golden brown.

Sweet Potato and Black Bean Tacos

Ingredients:

- 2 medium sweet potatoes, peeled and cubed
- 1 can black beans, rinsed and drained
- 1 teaspoon cumin
- 1 teaspoon paprika
- Salt and pepper to taste
- Corn tortillas
- Optional toppings: avocado, cilantro, lime juice

Instructions:

1. Preheat oven to 425°F (220°C).
2. Toss sweet potatoes with olive oil, cumin, paprika, salt, and pepper. Spread on a baking sheet.
3. Roast for 25-30 minutes until tender.
4. In a pan, warm black beans over medium heat.
5. Assemble tacos with roasted sweet potatoes, black beans, and desired toppings.

Mashed Sweet Potatoes with Garlic

Ingredients:

- 2 pounds sweet potatoes, peeled and cubed
- 4 cloves garlic, minced
- 1/4 cup unsalted butter
- 1/4 cup milk
- Salt and pepper to taste

Instructions:

1. Boil sweet potatoes in salted water until tender, about 15-20 minutes. Drain.
2. In a pan, melt butter over medium heat and sauté garlic until fragrant.
3. Mash sweet potatoes and mix in garlic, milk, salt, and pepper until creamy.

Sweet Potato and Kale Frittata

Ingredients:

- 1 medium sweet potato, peeled and diced
- 2 cups kale, chopped
- 6 eggs
- 1/4 cup milk
- 1/2 teaspoon salt
- 1/4 teaspoon pepper
- Olive oil for cooking

Instructions:

1. Preheat oven to 375°F (190°C).
2. In a skillet, heat olive oil over medium heat. Add sweet potato and cook until tender.
3. Stir in kale and cook until wilted.
4. In a bowl, whisk eggs, milk, salt, and pepper. Pour over the vegetables.
5. Cook until edges set, then transfer to the oven and bake until fully set, about 10-15 minutes.

Sweet Potato Quinoa Bowl

Ingredients:

- 1 cup quinoa, rinsed
- 2 cups water
- 2 medium sweet potatoes, cubed
- 1 can black beans, rinsed and drained
- 1/4 cup feta cheese
- Olive oil, salt, and pepper

Instructions:

1. Preheat oven to 425°F (220°C).
2. Toss sweet potatoes with olive oil, salt, and pepper. Roast for 25-30 minutes.
3. In a pot, bring water to a boil and add quinoa. Reduce heat, cover, and simmer for 15 minutes.
4. In a bowl, combine quinoa, black beans, roasted sweet potatoes, and top with feta.

Roasted Sweet Potato Salad with Feta

Ingredients:

- 2 medium sweet potatoes, cubed
- 1 tablespoon olive oil
- Salt and pepper to taste
- 4 cups mixed greens
- 1/4 cup feta cheese
- 1/4 cup walnuts, toasted
- Balsamic vinaigrette for dressing

Instructions:

1. Preheat oven to 425°F (220°C).
2. Toss sweet potatoes with olive oil, salt, and pepper. Roast for 25-30 minutes.
3. In a bowl, combine greens, roasted sweet potatoes, feta, and walnuts. Drizzle with balsamic vinaigrette before serving.

Sweet Potato and Chickpea Curry

Ingredients:

- 1 medium sweet potato, peeled and diced
- 1 can chickpeas, rinsed and drained
- 1 can coconut milk
- 1 tablespoon curry powder
- 1 teaspoon ginger, grated
- Salt to taste
- Fresh cilantro for garnish

Instructions:

1. In a pot, combine sweet potato, chickpeas, coconut milk, curry powder, ginger, and salt.
2. Bring to a simmer and cook until sweet potatoes are tender, about 20 minutes.
3. Serve warm, garnished with fresh cilantro.

Sweet Potato Gnocchi with Sage Butter

Ingredients:

- 2 medium sweet potatoes, baked and peeled
- 1 ½ cups all-purpose flour
- 1 egg, beaten
- 1 teaspoon salt
- 1/4 cup unsalted butter
- 8-10 fresh sage leaves
- Parmesan cheese for serving

Instructions:

1. In a bowl, mash the baked sweet potatoes until smooth. Mix in the egg and salt.
2. Gradually add flour, mixing until a soft dough forms. Divide into sections and roll into ropes; cut into bite-sized pieces.
3. Bring a pot of salted water to a boil. Cook gnocchi until they float, about 2-3 minutes. Remove and set aside.
4. In a skillet, melt butter over medium heat. Add sage leaves and cook until crisp.
5. Toss gnocchi in the sage butter and serve with Parmesan cheese.

Sweet Potato and Bacon Hash

Ingredients:

- 2 medium sweet potatoes, diced
- 4 strips bacon, chopped
- 1 small onion, diced
- 1 bell pepper, diced
- 2 eggs (optional)
- Salt and pepper to taste
- Fresh parsley for garnish

Instructions:

1. In a skillet, cook bacon until crispy. Remove and set aside, leaving the drippings in the pan.
2. Add sweet potatoes, onion, and bell pepper to the skillet. Cook until sweet potatoes are tender, about 15-20 minutes.
3. If desired, make two wells in the hash and crack an egg into each. Cover and cook until eggs are set.
4. Stir in cooked bacon, season with salt and pepper, and garnish with parsley before serving.

Sweet Potato Fries with Chipotle Mayo

Ingredients:

- 2 large sweet potatoes, cut into fries
- 2 tablespoons olive oil
- 1 teaspoon paprika
- Salt to taste
- 1/2 cup mayonnaise
- 1 tablespoon chipotle in adobo sauce, minced
- 1 teaspoon lime juice

Instructions:

1. Preheat oven to 425°F (220°C). Toss sweet potato fries with olive oil, paprika, and salt. Spread on a baking sheet.
2. Bake for 25-30 minutes, turning halfway, until crispy.
3. In a bowl, mix mayonnaise, chipotle, and lime juice for the dip.
4. Serve fries with chipotle mayo.

Stuffed Sweet Potatoes with Spinach and Feta

Ingredients:

- 4 medium sweet potatoes
- 2 cups fresh spinach
- 1/2 cup feta cheese, crumbled
- 1 tablespoon olive oil
- Salt and pepper to taste

Instructions:

1. Preheat oven to 400°F (200°C). Pierce sweet potatoes with a fork and bake for 45-60 minutes until tender.
2. In a skillet, heat olive oil and sauté spinach until wilted. Season with salt and pepper. Stir in feta cheese.
3. Once sweet potatoes are done, cut them open and fluff the insides with a fork.
4. Stuff the sweet potatoes with the spinach and feta mixture and serve warm.

Sweet Potato Soup with Coconut Milk

Ingredients:

- 2 medium sweet potatoes, peeled and diced
- 1 onion, chopped
- 2 cloves garlic, minced
- 4 cups vegetable broth
- 1 can coconut milk
- 1 tablespoon curry powder
- Salt and pepper to taste

Instructions:

1. In a large pot, sauté onion and garlic until translucent. Add diced sweet potatoes and cook for a few minutes.
2. Stir in vegetable broth and curry powder. Bring to a boil, then reduce heat and simmer until sweet potatoes are tender, about 15-20 minutes.
3. Blend the soup until smooth. Stir in coconut milk and season with salt and pepper. Heat through and serve.

Sweet Potato Pancakes

Ingredients:

- 1 cup mashed sweet potatoes
- 1 cup all-purpose flour
- 1 teaspoon baking powder
- 1/2 teaspoon baking soda
- 1/2 teaspoon cinnamon
- 1/2 cup milk
- 1 egg
- Butter or oil for cooking

Instructions:

1. In a bowl, mix mashed sweet potatoes, flour, baking powder, baking soda, and cinnamon.
2. In another bowl, whisk together milk and egg. Combine with the dry ingredients until just mixed.
3. Heat a skillet over medium heat and add butter or oil. Pour in batter to form pancakes and cook until bubbles form. Flip and cook until golden brown.
4. Serve with maple syrup or your favorite toppings.

Sweet Potato and Lentil Stew

Ingredients:

- 1 medium sweet potato, diced
- 1 cup lentils, rinsed
- 1 onion, chopped
- 2 carrots, diced
- 3 cloves garlic, minced
- 4 cups vegetable broth
- 1 teaspoon cumin
- 1 teaspoon thyme
- Salt and pepper to taste

Instructions:

1. In a pot, sauté onion, carrots, and garlic until soft. Add sweet potatoes and lentils, stirring for a few minutes.
2. Pour in vegetable broth and season with cumin, thyme, salt, and pepper. Bring to a boil.
3. Reduce heat and simmer until lentils and sweet potatoes are tender, about 25-30 minutes.
4. Adjust seasoning as needed and serve warm.

Sweet Potato Gratin with Gruyère

Ingredients:

- 2 large sweet potatoes, thinly sliced
- 1 cup heavy cream
- 1 cup Gruyère cheese, grated
- 2 cloves garlic, minced
- Salt and pepper to taste
- Fresh thyme for garnish

Instructions:

1. Preheat oven to 375°F (190°C). Grease a baking dish.
2. In a bowl, mix cream, garlic, salt, and pepper. Layer half of the sweet potato slices in the dish.
3. Pour half of the cream mixture over the sweet potatoes and sprinkle with half of the Gruyère cheese. Repeat layers.
4. Cover with foil and bake for 30 minutes. Remove foil and bake for an additional 20 minutes until golden and bubbly.
5. Garnish with fresh thyme before serving.

Sweet Potato Waffles with Maple Syrup

Ingredients:

- 1 cup mashed sweet potatoes
- 1 cup all-purpose flour
- 2 teaspoons baking powder
- 1/2 teaspoon cinnamon
- 1/4 teaspoon salt
- 1 cup milk
- 1 egg
- 2 tablespoons melted butter
- Maple syrup for serving

Instructions:

1. Preheat your waffle iron. In a bowl, mix mashed sweet potatoes, flour, baking powder, cinnamon, and salt.
2. In another bowl, whisk together milk, egg, and melted butter. Combine with the dry ingredients until just mixed.
3. Pour the batter into the preheated waffle iron and cook according to the manufacturer's instructions until golden brown.
4. Serve warm with maple syrup.

Sweet Potato and Apple Bake

Ingredients:

- 2 medium sweet potatoes, peeled and sliced
- 2 apples, peeled and sliced
- 1/4 cup brown sugar
- 1 teaspoon cinnamon
- 1/4 cup unsalted butter, melted
- 1/4 cup chopped pecans (optional)

Instructions:

1. Preheat oven to 350°F (175°C). In a baking dish, layer sweet potato and apple slices.
2. In a bowl, mix brown sugar, cinnamon, and melted butter. Pour over the layered sweet potatoes and apples.
3. Sprinkle with pecans if desired. Cover with foil and bake for 30 minutes. Remove foil and bake for an additional 15 minutes until tender.

Sweet Potato and Sausage Skillet

Ingredients:

- 2 medium sweet potatoes, diced
- 1 pound sausage (Italian or breakfast)
- 1 onion, chopped
- 2 cloves garlic, minced
- 1 bell pepper, diced
- Salt and pepper to taste
- Fresh parsley for garnish

Instructions:

1. In a large skillet, cook the sausage over medium heat until browned. Remove and set aside.
2. In the same skillet, add sweet potatoes, onion, garlic, and bell pepper. Cook until sweet potatoes are tender, about 15-20 minutes.
3. Stir in the cooked sausage, season with salt and pepper, and cook until heated through.
4. Garnish with fresh parsley before serving.

Sweet Potato Risotto with Parmesan

Ingredients:

- 1 cup Arborio rice
- 1 medium sweet potato, diced
- 1 onion, chopped
- 4 cups vegetable broth
- 1/2 cup white wine (optional)
- 1/2 cup grated Parmesan cheese
- 2 tablespoons olive oil
- Salt and pepper to taste
- Fresh sage for garnish

Instructions:

1. In a pot, heat vegetable broth and keep warm. In a separate pan, heat olive oil and sauté onion until translucent.
2. Add diced sweet potato and rice, stirring for a few minutes. Pour in white wine and cook until absorbed.
3. Gradually add warm broth, one ladle at a time, stirring frequently until absorbed. Continue until rice is creamy and al dente, about 20-25 minutes.
4. Stir in Parmesan cheese, season with salt and pepper, and garnish with fresh sage before serving.

Sweet Potato Pizza with Goat Cheese

Ingredients:

- 1 medium sweet potato, thinly sliced
- 1 pizza crust (store-bought or homemade)
- 1/2 cup goat cheese, crumbled
- 1/2 cup mozzarella cheese, shredded
- 2 tablespoons olive oil
- Fresh rosemary for garnish
- Salt and pepper to taste

Instructions:

1. Preheat oven according to pizza crust instructions. Roll out the crust on a baking sheet.
2. Arrange sweet potato slices on the crust. Drizzle with olive oil and season with salt and pepper.
3. Sprinkle goat cheese and mozzarella evenly over the top. Bake according to crust instructions until golden and bubbly.
4. Garnish with fresh rosemary before serving.

Sweet Potato and Corn Chowder

Ingredients:

- 2 medium sweet potatoes, peeled and diced
- 1 can corn (or 2 cups fresh)
- 1 onion, chopped
- 3 cups vegetable broth
- 1 cup coconut milk
- 1 teaspoon cumin
- Salt and pepper to taste
- Fresh cilantro for garnish

Instructions:

1. In a pot, sauté onion until soft. Add diced sweet potatoes, corn, vegetable broth, and cumin.
2. Bring to a boil, then reduce heat and simmer until sweet potatoes are tender, about 15-20 minutes.
3. Stir in coconut milk and season with salt and pepper. Blend slightly for a creamy texture if desired.
4. Serve warm, garnished with fresh cilantro.

Sweet Potato Hash Brown Casserole

Ingredients:

- 4 medium sweet potatoes, grated
- 1 cup shredded cheese (cheddar or your choice)
- 1/2 cup diced onion
- 2 eggs
- 1/2 cup milk
- 1 teaspoon garlic powder
- Salt and pepper to taste

Instructions:

1. Preheat oven to 375°F (190°C). In a bowl, combine grated sweet potatoes, onion, cheese, eggs, milk, garlic powder, salt, and pepper.
2. Transfer the mixture to a greased baking dish and spread evenly.
3. Bake for 30-35 minutes until the top is golden and set. Let cool slightly before serving.

Sweet Potato and Chicken Enchiladas

Ingredients:

- 2 medium sweet potatoes, peeled and diced
- 1 cup cooked chicken, shredded
- 1 cup enchilada sauce
- 1 cup cheese (cheddar or Mexican blend)
- 8 corn tortillas
- 1 teaspoon cumin
- Salt and pepper to taste
- Fresh cilantro for garnish

Instructions:

1. Preheat oven to 350°F (175°C). Cook diced sweet potatoes until tender, then mash and mix with cooked chicken, cumin, salt, and pepper.
2. Spread a little enchilada sauce on the bottom of a baking dish. Fill each tortilla with the sweet potato and chicken mixture, roll, and place seam side down in the dish.
3. Pour remaining enchilada sauce over the top and sprinkle with cheese. Bake for 20-25 minutes until cheese is bubbly.
4. Garnish with fresh cilantro before serving.

Sweet Potato Burgers with Avocado

Ingredients:

- 2 medium sweet potatoes, cooked and mashed
- 1 cup cooked quinoa
- 1/2 cup breadcrumbs
- 1/4 cup chopped green onions
- 1 teaspoon cumin
- Salt and pepper to taste
- 1 avocado, sliced
- Burger buns and toppings of choice

Instructions:

1. In a large bowl, combine mashed sweet potatoes, quinoa, breadcrumbs, green onions, cumin, salt, and pepper. Mix until well combined.
2. Form the mixture into patties. Heat a skillet over medium heat and lightly oil it.
3. Cook the patties for about 5 minutes on each side until golden brown.
4. Assemble the burgers with avocado slices and your favorite toppings.

Sweet Potato Salad with Apples and Pecans

Ingredients:

- 2 medium sweet potatoes, peeled and cubed
- 1 apple, diced
- 1/2 cup pecans, toasted
- 1/4 cup dried cranberries
- 2 tablespoons olive oil
- 1 tablespoon apple cider vinegar
- Salt and pepper to taste

Instructions:

1. Boil sweet potato cubes until tender, about 10-15 minutes. Drain and cool.
2. In a large bowl, combine cooked sweet potatoes, apple, pecans, and cranberries.
3. In a small bowl, whisk together olive oil, apple cider vinegar, salt, and pepper. Drizzle over the salad and toss gently.

Spicy Sweet Potato Hummus

Ingredients:

- 1 medium sweet potato, roasted and peeled
- 1 can chickpeas, drained and rinsed
- 2 tablespoons tahini
- 2 tablespoons olive oil
- 1 tablespoon lemon juice
- 1 teaspoon cayenne pepper (adjust to taste)
- Salt to taste

Instructions:

1. In a food processor, combine roasted sweet potato, chickpeas, tahini, olive oil, lemon juice, cayenne pepper, and salt.
2. Blend until smooth, adding water as needed to reach desired consistency.
3. Serve with pita chips or fresh veggies.

Sweet Potato Tater Tot Casserole

Ingredients:

- 2 cups sweet potato tater tots
- 1 pound ground beef or turkey
- 1 can cream of mushroom soup
- 1 cup shredded cheese (cheddar or your choice)
- 1 teaspoon garlic powder
- Salt and pepper to taste

Instructions:

1. Preheat oven to 375°F (190°C). In a skillet, cook ground beef or turkey until browned; drain excess fat.
2. In a baking dish, layer cooked meat, cream of mushroom soup, and garlic powder. Top with sweet potato tater tots and cheese.
3. Bake for 25-30 minutes until bubbly and golden.

Sweet Potato and Broccoli Stir-Fry

Ingredients:

- 2 medium sweet potatoes, peeled and diced
- 2 cups broccoli florets
- 2 tablespoons soy sauce
- 1 tablespoon sesame oil
- 2 cloves garlic, minced
- Sesame seeds for garnish

Instructions:

1. In a large skillet, heat sesame oil over medium heat. Add sweet potatoes and cook until tender, about 10 minutes.
2. Add broccoli and garlic, cooking for an additional 5 minutes.
3. Stir in soy sauce and cook for 2 more minutes. Garnish with sesame seeds before serving.

Sweet Potato and Shrimp Stir-Fry

Ingredients:

- 1 pound shrimp, peeled and deveined
- 2 medium sweet potatoes, peeled and julienned
- 1 bell pepper, sliced
- 2 tablespoons soy sauce
- 1 tablespoon ginger, minced
- 2 tablespoons olive oil

Instructions:

1. Heat olive oil in a skillet over medium-high heat. Add sweet potatoes and cook until slightly tender, about 5 minutes.
2. Add bell pepper and ginger, cooking for another 3-4 minutes.
3. Add shrimp and soy sauce, cooking until shrimp are pink and cooked through, about 4-5 minutes.

Sweet Potato Chilaquiles

Ingredients:

- 2 medium sweet potatoes, peeled and cubed
- 8 corn tortillas, cut into triangles
- 2 cups green salsa
- 1 cup shredded cheese (queso fresco or your choice)
- 2 eggs (optional)
- Fresh cilantro for garnish

Instructions:

1. Preheat oven to 375°F (190°C). Boil sweet potato cubes until tender, about 10 minutes, then drain.
2. In a baking dish, layer tortilla triangles, cooked sweet potatoes, green salsa, and cheese.
3. Bake for 15-20 minutes until cheese is bubbly. If using eggs, fry and place on top before serving. Garnish with cilantro.

Sweet Potato and Spinach Stuffed Shells

Ingredients:

- 12 jumbo pasta shells
- 1 medium sweet potato, cooked and mashed
- 2 cups fresh spinach
- 1 cup ricotta cheese
- 1/2 cup grated Parmesan cheese
- 2 cups marinara sauce
- Salt and pepper to taste

Instructions:

1. Preheat oven to 350°F (175°C). Cook pasta shells according to package instructions and drain.
2. In a bowl, combine mashed sweet potato, spinach, ricotta, Parmesan, salt, and pepper.
3. Stuff each pasta shell with the sweet potato mixture and place in a baking dish. Pour marinara sauce over the top and bake for 25 minutes.

Sweet Potato and Turkey Meatballs

Ingredients:

- 1 medium sweet potato, cooked and mashed
- 1 pound ground turkey
- 1/2 cup breadcrumbs
- 1/4 cup grated Parmesan cheese
- 1 egg
- 2 cloves garlic, minced
- 1 teaspoon Italian seasoning
- Salt and pepper to taste

Instructions:

1. Preheat oven to 400°F (200°C). In a bowl, combine mashed sweet potato, ground turkey, breadcrumbs, Parmesan, egg, garlic, Italian seasoning, salt, and pepper.
2. Form the mixture into meatballs and place them on a baking sheet lined with parchment paper.
3. Bake for 20-25 minutes or until cooked through.

Grilled Sweet Potato Skewers

Ingredients:

- 2 medium sweet potatoes, peeled and cubed
- 1 red bell pepper, cut into chunks
- 1 yellow bell pepper, cut into chunks
- 1 tablespoon olive oil
- 1 teaspoon smoked paprika
- Salt and pepper to taste
- Skewers

Instructions:

1. Preheat the grill to medium-high heat. In a bowl, toss sweet potatoes and bell peppers with olive oil, smoked paprika, salt, and pepper.
2. Thread the sweet potatoes and bell peppers onto skewers.
3. Grill for 15-20 minutes, turning occasionally, until sweet potatoes are tender and slightly charred.

Sweet Potato Sushi Rolls

Ingredients:

- 1 cup sushi rice
- 1 medium sweet potato, peeled and sliced into strips
- 1 avocado, sliced
- 4 sheets nori (seaweed)
- Rice vinegar
- Soy sauce for dipping

Instructions:

1. Cook sushi rice according to package instructions and mix with rice vinegar. Let cool.
2. Steam sweet potato strips until tender.
3. On a bamboo mat, lay a sheet of nori, spread a thin layer of rice, and add sweet potato and avocado strips.
4. Roll tightly and slice into pieces. Serve with soy sauce.

Sweet Potato Chocolate Chip Cookies

Ingredients:

- 1 medium sweet potato, cooked and mashed
- 1 cup brown sugar
- 1/2 cup butter, softened
- 1 egg
- 1 teaspoon vanilla extract
- 1 1/2 cups flour
- 1 teaspoon baking soda
- 1/2 cup chocolate chips

Instructions:

1. Preheat oven to 350°F (175°C). In a bowl, cream together mashed sweet potato, brown sugar, and butter. Beat in the egg and vanilla.
2. In another bowl, whisk together flour and baking soda. Gradually add to the sweet potato mixture. Stir in chocolate chips.
3. Drop spoonfuls onto a baking sheet and bake for 10-12 minutes.

Sweet Potato Pudding

Ingredients:

- 2 medium sweet potatoes, peeled and cubed
- 1/2 cup brown sugar
- 1/4 cup milk
- 1/4 cup butter, melted
- 1 teaspoon vanilla extract
- 1 teaspoon cinnamon
- Pinch of salt

Instructions:

1. Boil sweet potatoes until tender, then drain and mash. Preheat the oven to 350°F (175°C).
2. In a mixing bowl, combine mashed sweet potatoes, brown sugar, milk, melted butter, vanilla, cinnamon, and salt.
3. Pour into a baking dish and bake for 25-30 minutes until set.

Sweet Potato and Mushroom Risotto

Ingredients:

- 1 medium sweet potato, peeled and diced
- 1 cup Arborio rice
- 1 onion, chopped
- 4 cups vegetable broth
- 1 cup mushrooms, sliced
- 1/2 cup Parmesan cheese
- 2 tablespoons olive oil
- Salt and pepper to taste

Instructions:

1. In a pot, heat vegetable broth and keep it warm. In a separate pan, heat olive oil, add onion, and sauté until translucent.
2. Add mushrooms and sweet potato; cook until soft. Stir in Arborio rice and cook for 2 minutes.
3. Gradually add warm broth, one ladle at a time, stirring continuously until absorbed. Stir in Parmesan cheese and season with salt and pepper.

Sweet Potato and Green Bean Salad

Ingredients:

- 2 medium sweet potatoes, peeled and diced
- 2 cups green beans, trimmed
- 1/4 cup red onion, sliced
- 1/4 cup feta cheese, crumbled
- 2 tablespoons olive oil
- 1 tablespoon balsamic vinegar
- Salt and pepper to taste

Instructions:

1. Boil sweet potato cubes until tender, about 10 minutes, and blanch green beans for 3-4 minutes. Drain both and let cool.
2. In a bowl, combine sweet potatoes, green beans, red onion, and feta cheese. In a small bowl, whisk together olive oil, balsamic vinegar, salt, and pepper.
3. Drizzle the dressing over the salad and toss gently.

Sweet Potato Muffins

Ingredients:

- 1 medium sweet potato, cooked and mashed
- 1 cup flour
- 1/2 cup brown sugar
- 1/4 cup vegetable oil
- 1/2 cup milk
- 1 egg
- 1 teaspoon baking powder
- 1/2 teaspoon cinnamon

Instructions:

1. Preheat oven to 350°F (175°C) and line a muffin tin with liners. In a bowl, mix mashed sweet potato, sugar, oil, milk, and egg.
2. In another bowl, whisk together flour, baking powder, and cinnamon. Gradually add dry ingredients to the wet ingredients.
3. Fill muffin tins and bake for 20-25 minutes until a toothpick comes out clean.

Baked Sweet Potato and Egg Breakfast Bowls

Ingredients:

- 2 medium sweet potatoes, halved
- 4 eggs
- 1 avocado, sliced
- 1 cup spinach
- Olive oil
- Salt and pepper to taste
- Hot sauce (optional)

Instructions:

1. Preheat the oven to 400°F (200°C). Place sweet potato halves on a baking sheet, drizzle with olive oil, and season with salt and pepper. Bake for 25-30 minutes until tender.
2. In the last 10 minutes of baking, crack an egg into the center of each sweet potato half.
3. Once cooked, top with spinach and avocado slices. Drizzle with hot sauce if desired.

Sweet Potato Chocolate Brownies

Ingredients:

- 1 cup sweet potato puree (about 1 medium sweet potato)
- 1/2 cup almond butter
- 1/2 cup cocoa powder
- 1/4 cup maple syrup
- 2 eggs
- 1 teaspoon vanilla extract
- 1/2 teaspoon baking powder
- A pinch of salt

Instructions:

1. Preheat the oven to 350°F (175°C) and line an 8x8-inch baking dish with parchment paper.
2. In a bowl, mix sweet potato puree, almond butter, cocoa powder, maple syrup, eggs, vanilla, baking powder, and salt until smooth.
3. Pour the batter into the prepared dish and bake for 20-25 minutes. Let cool before slicing into squares.

Sweet Potato and Coconut Curry

Ingredients:

- 1 medium sweet potato, peeled and diced
- 1 can coconut milk
- 1 cup vegetable broth
- 1 onion, chopped
- 2 cloves garlic, minced
- 1 tablespoon curry powder
- 1 cup spinach
- Salt and pepper to taste
- Cooked rice for serving

Instructions:

1. In a large pot, heat a splash of oil and sauté onion and garlic until translucent. Add curry powder and stir for 1 minute.
2. Add sweet potatoes, coconut milk, and vegetable broth. Bring to a simmer and cook for 15-20 minutes until sweet potatoes are tender.
3. Stir in spinach and cook until wilted. Season with salt and pepper. Serve over cooked rice.

Sweet Potato and White Bean Chili

Ingredients:

- 1 medium sweet potato, peeled and diced
- 1 can white beans, drained and rinsed
- 1 can diced tomatoes
- 1 onion, chopped
- 2 cloves garlic, minced
- 1 tablespoon chili powder
- 1 teaspoon cumin
- 2 cups vegetable broth
- Olive oil
- Salt and pepper to taste

Instructions:

1. In a large pot, heat olive oil and sauté onion and garlic until soft. Add chili powder and cumin, stirring for 1 minute.
2. Add sweet potatoes, white beans, diced tomatoes, and vegetable broth. Bring to a boil, then reduce heat and simmer for 20-25 minutes until sweet potatoes are tender.
3. Season with salt and pepper before serving.

Sweet Potato and Cauliflower Tacos

Ingredients:

- 1 medium sweet potato, peeled and diced
- 1 small head of cauliflower, cut into florets
- 1 tablespoon olive oil
- 1 teaspoon chili powder
- Salt and pepper to taste
- Corn tortillas
- Toppings: avocado, cilantro, lime wedges

Instructions:

1. Preheat oven to 425°F (220°C). Toss sweet potatoes and cauliflower with olive oil, chili powder, salt, and pepper on a baking sheet.
2. Roast for 25-30 minutes until tender and slightly crispy.
3. Warm corn tortillas and fill with roasted sweet potatoes and cauliflower. Top with avocado, cilantro, and a squeeze of lime.

Sweet Potato and Zucchini Fritters

Ingredients:

- 1 medium sweet potato, grated
- 1 medium zucchini, grated
- 1/2 cup flour (or gluten-free alternative)
- 1 egg
- 1/4 cup green onions, chopped
- Salt and pepper to taste
- Olive oil for frying

Instructions:

1. In a bowl, combine grated sweet potato, zucchini, flour, egg, green onions, salt, and pepper until well mixed.
2. Heat olive oil in a skillet over medium heat. Drop spoonfuls of the mixture into the skillet and flatten slightly.
3. Cook for 3-4 minutes on each side until golden brown. Drain on paper towels and serve warm.

Sweet Potato and Brussels Sprouts Salad

Ingredients:

- 2 cups Brussels sprouts, halved
- 1 medium sweet potato, peeled and diced
- 2 tablespoons olive oil
- Salt and pepper to taste
- 1/4 cup feta cheese, crumbled
- 1/4 cup walnuts, chopped
- 2 tablespoons balsamic vinegar

Instructions:

1. Preheat the oven to 400°F (200°C). Toss Brussels sprouts and sweet potatoes with olive oil, salt, and pepper on a baking sheet. Roast for 25-30 minutes until tender.
2. In a large bowl, combine roasted vegetables with feta cheese and walnuts. Drizzle with balsamic vinegar and toss to combine.

Sweet Potato Mac and Cheese

Ingredients:

- 1 medium sweet potato, peeled and cubed
- 1 cup pasta (your choice)
- 1 cup cheddar cheese, shredded
- 1/2 cup milk
- 1/4 cup nutritional yeast (optional)
- 1 teaspoon garlic powder
- Salt and pepper to taste

Instructions:

1. Cook pasta according to package instructions. Drain and set aside.
2. In a pot, boil sweet potato cubes until tender. Drain and blend with milk, nutritional yeast, garlic powder, salt, and pepper until smooth.
3. Combine the sweet potato sauce with the cooked pasta and stir in cheddar cheese until melted. Serve warm.

Sweet Potato and Roasted Beet Salad

Ingredients:

- 1 medium sweet potato, peeled and diced
- 2 medium beets, peeled and diced
- 2 tablespoons olive oil
- Salt and pepper to taste
- 4 cups mixed greens
- 1/4 cup goat cheese, crumbled
- 1/4 cup walnuts, chopped
- Balsamic vinaigrette for dressing

Instructions:

1. Preheat the oven to 400°F (200°C). Toss sweet potatoes and beets with olive oil, salt, and pepper on a baking sheet. Roast for 25-30 minutes until tender.
2. In a large bowl, combine mixed greens, roasted sweet potatoes, beets, goat cheese, and walnuts. Drizzle with balsamic vinaigrette before serving.

Sweet Potato Chocolate Mousse

Ingredients:

- 1 cup sweet potato puree (about 1 medium sweet potato)
- 1/2 cup cocoa powder
- 1/4 cup maple syrup (adjust to taste)
- 1 teaspoon vanilla extract
- A pinch of salt
- Whipped cream for serving (optional)

Instructions:

1. In a blender, combine sweet potato puree, cocoa powder, maple syrup, vanilla extract, and salt. Blend until smooth and creamy.
2. Chill in the refrigerator for at least 30 minutes before serving. Serve with whipped cream if desired.

www.ingramcontent.com/pod-product-compliance
Lightning Source LLC
LaVergne TN
LVHW081504060526
838201LV00056BA/2931